AMERICA'S INDUSTRIAL SOCIETY IN THE 19TH CENTURY ™

Possibilities and Problems in America's New Urban Centers

The Rise of Cities

Suzanne J. Murdico

rosen central
Primary Source™

The Rosen Publishing Group, Inc., New York

For my good friends, Zaan and Kelly Gast

Published in 2004 by The Rosen Publishing Group
29 East 21st Street, New York, NY 10010

First Edition

Library of Congress Cataloging-in-Publication Data

Murdico, Suzanne J.
Possibilities and problems in America's new urban centers: the rise of cities/Suzanne J. Murdico.
   p. cm.—(America's industrial society in the nineteenth century)
Includes bibliographical references (p.) and index.
ISBN 0-8239-4031-4 (library binding)
ISBN 0-8239-4277-5 (paperback)
6-pack ISBN 0-8239-4289-9
1. Cities and towns—United States—Growth—Juvenile literature. 2. Urbanization—United States—Juvenile literature.
I. Title. II. Series.

HT123 .M794 2003
307.76'0973--dc21

2002155651

Manufactured in the United States of America

On the cover: Large cover image: Map of Boston Highlands, Massachusetts. First row (from left to right): steamship docked at a landing; Tammany Hall on election night 1859; map showing U.S. railroad routes in 1883; detail of banknote, 1822, Bank of the Commonwealth of Kentucky; People's Party (Populist) Convention in Columbus, Nebraska, 1890; Republican ticket, 1865. Second row (from left to right): William McKinley gives a campaign speech in 1896; parade banner of the Veterans of the Haymarket Riot; Alexander Graham Bell's sketch of the telephone, c. 1876; public declaration of the government's ability to crush monopolies; city planners' illustration of Stockton, California; railroad construction camp, Nebraska, 1889.

Photo credits: Cover, p. 6 © Library of Congress, Geography and Map Division; pp. 5, 18, 25 © Culver Pictures, Inc.; p. 9 © Hulton/Archive/Getty Images; pp. 10, 11, 13 Courtesy of *New York in the Nineteenth Century*, Dover Publications, Inc.; pp. 15, 21, 22 © Library of Congress, Prints and Photographs Division; p. 19 © Bettmann/Corbis; p. 26 © Corbis.

Designer: Tahara Hasan; **Editor:** Mark Beyer; **Photo Researcher:** Peter Tomlinson

Contents

1

From Rural to Urban

Before 1800, the United States was a rural society. Most people lived on farms, where they raised crops. Modern farm machinery had yet to be invented. So, farmers used farm animals to help with the planting and harvesting. All of the family members helped, too. They also made their own cloth by spinning and weaving thread. Then they used this cloth to make clothing, sheets, and other items. Tools and furniture were also made by hand.

By the early 1800s, farming was still an important part of the U.S. economy. The invention of new farm machines, however, made it much easier and faster to plant and harvest crops. This meant that fewer workers were needed on the farm. With more free time, farm workers were able to focus on making cloth, tools, and other products. They sold or traded these goods for other items that they needed.

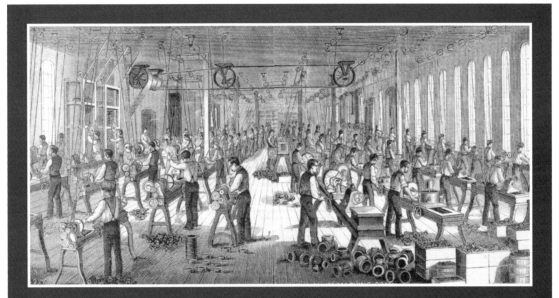

Thousands of farmers moved to the cities in the 19th century. Factories offered jobs for thousands who were underemployed. When people moved to the cities, they found out that the factories were bad places to work. This 1881 engraving shows dozens of workers in a single room. The machines they worked on were dangerous. Pay was low. Injury was common.

During this time, the United States was becoming an industrialized nation. The Industrial Revolution brought major changes in the way people lived and worked. The steam engine and other inventions provided new sources of power. That power was then used to run machines. With power-driven machines, goods could be produced quickly and cheaply. This process became known as mass

Cities became crowded quickly as people moved in from the farms. This map illustration of Boston Highlands, Massachusetts, shows poor 19th-century city planning. Many slums grew from such crowded conditions. Most factory workers did not earn enough money to pay to live in safe neighborhoods.

production. The mass production of goods meant that people no longer needed to make everything by hand.

Many skilled craftspeople now found themselves without jobs. However, a large number of workers were needed to operate the machines used for mass production. To earn money, many people took jobs working in factories. These factories were usually located in cities. Since most people had to walk to work, they moved to the city. As more people moved into cities, the United States changed from a rural society to an urban society.

During the early 1800s, most U.S. cities were located east of the Mississippi River. The largest cities, including New York, Boston, and Philadelphia, were in the Northeast. Cities were usually found along waterways, such as large rivers, or along the Atlantic Ocean. These locations allowed goods produced in the city to be shipped to other areas. Railroads provided another method of transportation. They ran between cities and allowed products and people to get from one place to another.

In 1880, about 28 percent of the U.S. population lived in cities. Just twenty years later, that number had climbed to 40 percent. People were coming to the United States from far-off places. They flocked to the cities to find new places to live and work.

2
Life in the City

People moved to cities for a variety of reasons. There were many things to see and do in cities. They had theaters, museums, and libraries. People who lived there could eat in fine restaurants. Stores carried a wide range of products for sale. And, of course, many jobs could be found in the city.

Cities grew very quickly during the Industrial Revolution—sometimes too quickly. There were not enough homes for everyone to live in. The streets became crowded with people and horses. Builders couldn't keep up with rising construction demands. Stores had trouble keeping enough products on the shelves.

Industrial cities had other problems, too. The more people who lived in the city, the more trash they created. Trash and other wastes piled up, creating health risks. Factories also caused health problems. They created air

The Lower East Side of New York City was crowded with immigrants. They worked for very low wages. Many lived in tiny apartments that were dirty and rat-infested. Only when unions demanded help for the workers did people begin to live better lives.

pollution by spewing smoke and other fumes into the air. Factories also created water pollution by releasing chemical waste into rivers and streams.

In most cities two very distinct social classes could be found. One social class included people who worked long hours in factories or at other low-paying jobs. These people were members of the working class. At the other end of the scale was the upper class. Members of this social class were very wealthy. They often owned factories or other businesses.

Members of these two social classes lived in different parts of the city. They also led very different lives. Rich people wore fancy clothes and traveled in horse-drawn carriages. They

Cities rarely helped the poor. Often charitable organizations were the poor's only hope. This engraving shows the government of New York City giving out free coal to the poor during the cold winter of 1877.

lived in large houses with many rooms. Poor people usually made their own clothes and walked wherever they needed to go. They often lived in a few rooms within small, crowded apartments called tenements.

By the mid-1800s, railroads reached cities like Chicago and St. Louis in the Midwest. The U.S. population then began to spread from east to west. Between 1840 and 1890, Chicago's population climbed from four thousand to more than one million. This westward growth helped to relieve

City governments began to take better care of their citizens by the 1890s. In New York City, firefighter hook and ladder teams raced to many small daily fires. Their ladders reached up to ninety feet when put together. This helped save many people's lives.

some of the overcrowded conditions in northeastern cities. By 1869, rail lines stretched all the way across the United States. This helped to promote the development of cities in California and other places on the West Coast.

Life in the cities began to improve in the second half of the nineteenth century. Cities worked hard to make their streets safer. They hired police officers and firefighters to help people and protect them from harm. Cities also took steps to make streets cleaner and healthier. They hired garbage collectors to pick up trash.

3
In Search of a Better Life

The Industrial Revolution saw a huge increase in the number of people living in the United States. In 1800, the United States population was only about 5 million. By 1880, that number had risen to more than 50 million. At the turn of the twentieth century, 76 million people were living in the United States.

One reason for this amazing growth was the rise in the number of immigrants. Between 1880 and 1900, more than 9 million immigrants entered the United States. Many of these people came from countries in northern and western Europe, including Ireland and Germany. By the end of the nineteenth century, more immigrants began coming from southern and eastern Europe. These countries included Italy, Poland, and Hungary.

Most immigrants came to America in search of a better life. Many wanted to avoid the starvation, poverty, and

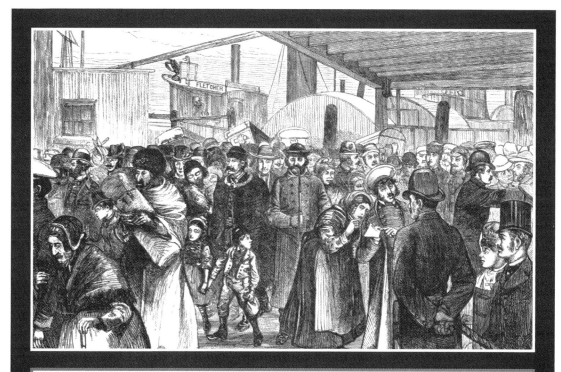

Most European immigrants came through New York City in the late 1800s. Before Ellis Island, immigrants registered at Castle Garden. Forty percent of the 180,000 immigrants who arrived in 1879 stayed in eastern cities.

unemployment in their homelands. Some left to escape war, overpopulation, or religious persecution. They wanted to be free to practice whatever religion they chose. Most immigrants saw America as a land of opportunity. They hoped to find jobs that would allow them to provide food, clothing, and shelter for their families.

Andrew Carnegie

Not all immigrants ended up as poor factory workers. Andrew Carnegie (1835–1919) was a Scottish immigrant who became a steel tycoon. During his time, he was one of the richest people in the world. He used his great fortune to help others and to promote worthwhile causes.

At the age of twelve, Carnegie immigrated with his family to the United States from Scotland. Early in his career, Carnegie held various jobs. They included cotton mill worker, clerk, and telegraph operator. Carnegie recognized that there would be an increasing need for steel. So, he decided to open a steel mill. His steel company grew and earned millions of dollars. In 1901, Carnegie sold the company and retired with a fortune of about $500 million.

Carnegie didn't believe in charity, but he did believe in helping people to help themselves. He gave about $350 million to a variety of causes. Much of this money was used to build several thousand libraries around the world. It was also used to found several schools and a concert hall.

Even though Andrew Carnegie was born poor, he had no sympathy for factory workers. He paid low wages and demanded long hours. When some of his workers went on strike in 1892, Carnegie's managers called in strike breakers. The fight that followed killed ten people. Ultimately, Carnegie won against the strikers, and factory conditions did not change.

Factory owners needed many workers to operate the machines that mass-produced goods. They hired the immigrants who had come to the United States in search of work. Relatives and friends still in Europe heard about the great number of jobs available. Many of them also decided to immigrate to America. More and more immigrants moved into the cities in search of work. The cities started to become very crowded.

For many immigrants, life in the United States didn't turn out to be all that they had hoped for. Factory jobs required long hours and hard work but paid low wages. Immigrants were often willing to work for less money than other factory workers. They needed to support their families and could not afford to return to their homelands. Some factory owners took advantage of that fact and paid immigrants less than other workers. Most factory owners earned hefty profits but rarely shared the wealth with their employees.

4
Working in Factories

During the Industrial Revolution, factories were built in cities throughout the United States. Some of these factories were textile mills, where workers used machines to make fabrics. Other factories produced iron or steel. Still other factories manufactured guns or farm equipment.

Jobs in factories were easy to find. Working conditions in those factories were very different from conditions in factories today. Back then, factories were often dirty, unsafe, and poorly lit. They were also hot and stuffy, with very little fresh air. These conditions sometimes caused workers to become sick. The lack of safety equipment meant that workers were frequently hurt on the job.

Most factory employees worked ten to twelve hours each day, six days a week. Sunday was their only day off. The work was very boring. They performed the same task, over and over, day after day. Workers were rarely

Factory work was loud and dangerous throughout America's Industrial Revolution. People were forced to work quickly on unsafe machines. If they didn't produce enough work, they were fired. This increased the risk for many accidents. Workers suffered broken hands and arms because of the dangerous machines.

allowed to take a break. For their efforts, they earned low wages and few, if any, benefits.

Today, you would never see children working in a factory. During the Industrial Revolution, however, child labor was common. At the time, there were no laws requiring that

children attend school. Many families were very poor. They needed the extra income their children could earn by working rather than going to school. Some children sold newspapers or matches on street corners. Others worked as servants for wealthy families. Many children, often as young as six years old, worked in factories.

The worst part of factory work was the presence of children. Many families had to have all members working in order to survive in expensive cities. Children often worked as many hours as their parents. Notice that one of the boys shown working on a spindle machine is not wearing any shoes.

These children labored alongside adults. For performing certain tasks, a child's tiny fingers were the ideal size. Unlike adults, the children were small enough to clean under the machines. They worked the same long hours as adults yet received even less money. Children working in factories earned about $2 per week.

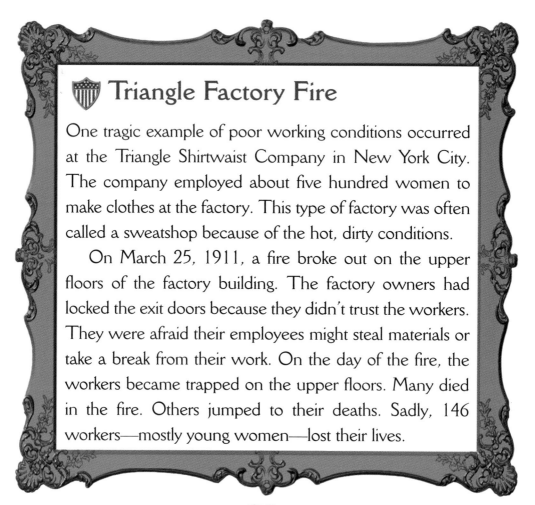

Triangle Factory Fire

One tragic example of poor working conditions occurred at the Triangle Shirtwaist Company in New York City. The company employed about five hundred women to make clothes at the factory. This type of factory was often called a sweatshop because of the hot, dirty conditions.

On March 25, 1911, a fire broke out on the upper floors of the factory building. The factory owners had locked the exit doors because they didn't trust the workers. They were afraid their employees might steal materials or take a break from their work. On the day of the fire, the workers became trapped on the upper floors. Many died in the fire. Others jumped to their deaths. Sadly, 146 workers—mostly young women—lost their lives.

Factory workers were sometimes locked in the rooms in which they worked. This caused one of the greatest tragedies of the Industrial Revolution. A fire at New York City's Triangle Shirtwaist Company in 1911 killed 146 young women in less than fifteen minutes. Firefighters discovered that exit doors had been locked on the ninth floor.

Meanwhile, factory owners and big businesses were making a great deal of money. Many became very rich due in large part to the hard work of their employees. There's a

Firefighters at the Triangle fire look into a hole in the sidewalk outside the factory. They are looking for survivors. Few workers from the ninth floor survived. The Triangle fire brought the dangers of factory work to public attention.

saying that: "The rich get richer, and the poor get poorer." That was surely true during the Industrial Revolution.

Most factory owners seemed not to care much about employees' rights. Factory workers had few choices and nowhere to turn for help. Workers who became sick or were injured on the job had to pay for their own doctors' bills. They didn't receive wages for days that they didn't work. Those who complained about poor working conditions risked being fired. Workers needed a way to band together and fight for their rights.

5
A Brighter Future

By the second half of the 1800s, workers had become fed up. They were tired of the terrible working conditions in factories and mills. They didn't like that employers were more interested in company profits than in workers' health and safety. The workers decided to form labor unions. These groups were organized to fight for workers' rights. Labor unions demanded better pay, shorter workdays, and safer working conditions.

Skilled workers, including carpenters and printers, developed the first unions in the United States. These citywide groups were formed to fight for higher wages. In the mid-1800s, ironworkers, shoemakers, and members of other skilled trades started nationwide unions. These labor unions would threaten to strike, or stop working, if their demands weren't met.

Labor unions had power in numbers. They knew that employers wouldn't be able to produce goods if all their employees stopped working. Of course, factory owners and big businesses didn't like the unions. They didn't want to pay their workers more money or let them work shorter hours. That would mean less profit for the business. They tried to stop union activity and prevent strikes.

Pullman Strike

One of the most violent labor strikes was the Pullman Strike, in 1894. The strike involved the Pullman Company and the American Railway Union (ARU). Pullman manufactured railroad cars. The ARU was a union of railroad workers led by Eugene V. Debs.

The strike began when Pullman employees protested a wage cut. ARU members wanted to show their support for the Pullman workers. So they refused to haul the Pullman railroad cars. The railroad strike created problems because it held up trains that carried mail. The U.S. government sent troops to stop the strike. Violence broke out. Debs and other union leaders were arrested and sent to prison.

The Pullman Railroad strike in 1894 caused a violent clash between workers striking and paid strike breakers. This photo captures the damage caused by fire set to freight cars in Chicago. Strikers had demanded safer working conditions, better pay, and payment to injured workers.

It took many years before the labor movement became widely accepted. In the 1930s, the U.S. government passed laws requiring employers to bargain with labor unions. This led to a better way of life for workers. Today's workers earn more money, work fewer hours, and have a safer

Some states outlawed child labor by the early 1900s. Unions made politicians understand that education was the only way to improve people's lives. Children had to be able to go to school. Here, children in Homestead, Pennsylvania, walk to school. Behind them, steel mills spew smoke into the air.

work environment. They also receive more benefits, such as paid vacations and sick days.

Eventually, life also improved for children. In the 1930s, the U.S. government passed a law that included rules about child labor. Children who were fourteen and fifteen could work only in certain jobs and only before or after school. Children aged sixteen and older could work at any jobs except those considered dangerous. The law also stated that employers must pay children the standard minimum wage.

In some ways, better pay for workers benefited both workers and businesses. Mass production methods had cut the cost of manufacturing goods. This allowed products to be sold at lower prices. Higher earnings along with these lower prices enabled workers to buy more. This greater demand for goods led to an increase in production. New factories were built to meet these demands, thus creating new jobs. This type of economic cycle continues to this day.

Glossary

economy (ih-KAH-nuh-mee) The management of money and resources.

employee (em-PLOY-ee) Someone who is paid to work for a person or business.

factory (FAK-tuh-ree) Building where goods are produced.

harvesting (HAR-vest-ing) The gathering of a crop when it is ripe.

immigrant (IH-muh-grint) A person who moves to a different country to live.

income (IN-kum) Money received for work.

industrialize (in-DUS-tree-ul-ize) To develop industries as a vital part of a country's economy.

labor union (LAY-ber YOON-yun) A group of workers joined to protect their rights on the job.

manufacture (man-yoo-FAK-chur) To make something by hand or by machine.

mass production (MASS pruh-DUK-shun) The making of goods in large quantities.

overpopulation (**OH-ver-pahp-yoo-LAY-shun**) Too many people in a given area.

persecution (**PER-sih-KYOO-shun**) Poor treatment because of a person's or group's beliefs.

pollution (**puh-LOO-shun**) The act of making something dirty.

population (**pahp-yoo-LAY-shun**) The people who live in a particular area.

poverty (**PAH-ver-tee**) The condition of being poor.

profit (**PRAH-fit**) Money earned by a business

rural (**RUR-ul**) Having to do with farming.

strike (**STRYK**) A work stoppage by a group of workers as a way to demand changes from their employer.

tenement (**TEN-uh-ment**) A small, crowded apartment.

textile (**TEK-styl**) Woven fabric.

transportation (**TRANZ-por-TAY-shun**) The action of carrying people or goods from one place to another.

tycoon (**ty-KOON**) A person who has earned great wealth and power in a certain business or industry.

unemployment (**UN-em-PLOY-ment**) The state of being out of work.

urban (**UR-buhn**) Having to do with cities and towns.

wages (**WAYJ-ez**) Payment for work performed.

Web Sites

Due to the changing nature of Internet links, the Rosen Publishing Group, Inc., has developed an online list of Web sites related to the subject of this book. This site is updated regularly. Please use this link to access the list:

http://www.rosenlinks.com/aistc/ppanuc

Primary Source Image List

Cover and page 6: Drawn map of Boston Highlands, Massachusetts, 1888. The O. H. Bailey & Co. It is currently housed at the Library of Congress, Washington, DC.

Page 5: 1881 etching, "Main Machine Room" in *Scientific American.*

Page 9: 1898 photographic print of outdoor market on Orchard Street, Lower East Side, New York City. It is currently housed at the Museum of the City of New York, New York, NY.

Page 10: 1877 engraving by C. A. Keetels of coal distribution to New York's poor, appearing in *Harper's Weekly.*

Page 11: 1891 engraving by T. de Thulstrup of a NYC firefighter hook and ladder company, appearing in *Harper's Weekly.*

Page 13: Illustration by A. B. Shults of immigrants landing at Castle Garden, appearing in *Harper's Weekly,* 1881.

Page 15: Photograph of Andrew Carnegie by B. L. H. Dobbs, circa 1896. It is currently housed at the Library of Congress, Washington DC.

Page 18: Photograph of interior of cotton mill in South Carolina, circa 1890.

Page 19: Nineteenth-century photograph by Lewis Hines of children working in cotton mill.

Page 21: 1911 photographic print of bodies outside Triangle Shirtwaist Company. It is currently housed at the Library of Congress, Washington, DC.

Page 22: 1911 photographic print of NYC firemen searching for victims of the Triangle Shirtwaist Company fire. It is currently housed at the Library of Congress, Washington, DC.

Page 25: 1894 photographic print by R. D. Cleveland of the Pullman Railroad strike in Chicago.

Page 26: Photographic print of children going to school in Homestead, Pennsylvania, circa 1900.

Index

About the Author

Suzanne J. Murdico is a freelance writer who has authored numerous books for children and teens. She lives in Florida with her husband, Vinnie, and their cat, Zuzu.